J

by Iain Gray

Lang**Syne**

PUBLISHING

WRITING *to* REMEMBER

Lang**Syne**

PUBLISHING

WRITING *to* REMEMBER

Strathclyde Business Centre
120 Carstairs Street, Glasgow G40 4JD
Tel: 0141 554 9944 Fax: 0141 554 9955
E-mail: info@scottish-memories.co.uk
www.langsyneshop.co.uk

Design by Dorothy Meikle
Printed by Hay Nisbet Press, Glasgow
© Lang Syne Publishers Ltd 2008

ISBN 1-85217-258-4

Joyce

MOTTO:
Death, or life with honour.

CREST:
A lion rampant.

NAME variations include:
Seoighe *(Gaelic)*, Joyes,
Joy, Joice, Joisce, Joss, Joicey.

Chapter one:
Origins of Irish surnames

**According to an old saying, there are two types of Irish –
those who actually are Irish and those who wish they were.**

This sentiment is only one example of the allure that the
high romance and drama of the proud nation's history holds
for thousands of people scattered across the world today.

It's a sad fact, however, that the vast majority of Irish
surnames are found far beyond Irish shores, rather than on
the Emerald Isle itself.

The population stood at around eight million souls in
1841, but today it stands at fewer than six million.

This is mainly a tragic consequence of the potato
famine, also known as the Great Hunger, which devastated
Ireland between 1845 and 1849.

The Irish peasantry had become almost wholly reliant
for basic sustenance on the potato, first introduced from the
Americas in the seventeenth century.

When the crop was hit by a blight, at least 800,000
people starved to death while an estimated two million
others were forced to seek a new life far from their native
shores – particularly in America, Canada, and Australia.

The effects of the potato blight continued until about
1851, by which time a firm pattern of emigration had
become established.

Ireland's loss, however, was to the gain of the countries in which the immigrants settled, contributing enormously, as their descendants do today, to the well being of the nations in which their forefathers settled.

But those who were forced through dire circumstance to establish a new life in foreign parts never forgot their roots, or the proud heritage and traditions of the land that gave them birth.

Nor do their descendants.

It is a heritage that is inextricably bound up in the colourful variety of Irish names themselves – and the origin and history of these names forms an integral part of the vibrant drama that is the nation's history, one of both glorious fortune and tragic misfortune.

This history is well documented, and one of the most important and fascinating of the earliest sources are *The Annals of the Four Masters*, compiled between 1632 and 1636 by four friars at the Franciscan Monastery in County Donegal.

Compiled from earlier sources, and purporting to go back to the Biblical Deluge, much of the material takes in the mythological origins and history of Ireland and the Irish.

This includes tales of successive waves of invaders and settlers such as the Fomorians, the Partholonians, the Nemedians, the Fir Bolgs, the Tuatha De Danann, and the Laigain.

Of particular interest are the *Milesian Genealogies*,

because the majority of Irish clans today claim a descent from either Heremon, Ir, or Heber – three of the sons of Milesius, a king of what is now modern day Spain.

These sons invaded Ireland in the second millennium B.C, apparently in fulfilment of a mysterious prophecy received by their father.

This Milesian lineage is said to have ruled Ireland for nearly 3,000 years, until the island came under the sway of England's King Henry II in 1171 following what is known as the Cambro-Norman invasion.

This is an important date not only in Irish history in general, but for the effect the invasion subsequently had for Irish surnames.

'Cambro' comes from the Welsh, and 'Cambro-Norman' describes those Welsh knights of Norman origin who invaded Ireland.

But they were invaders who stayed, inter-marrying with the native Irish population and founding their own proud dynasties that bore Cambro-Norman names such as Archer, Barbour, Brannagh, Fitzgerald, Fitzgibbon, Fleming, Joyce, Plunkett, and Walsh – to name only a few.

These 'Cambro-Norman' surnames that still flourish throughout the world today form one of the three main categories in which Irish names can be placed – those of Gaelic-Irish, Cambro-Norman, and Anglo-Irish.

Previous to the Cambro-Norman invasion of the twelfth century, and throughout the earlier invasions and settlement of those wild bands of sea rovers known as the Vikings in the eighth and ninth centuries, the population of the island was relatively small, and it was normal for a person to be identified through the use of only a forename.

But as population gradually increased and there were many more people with the same forename, surnames were adopted to distinguish one person, or one community, from another.

Individuals identified themselves with their own particular tribe, or 'tuath', and this tribe – that also became known as a clann, or clan – took its name from some distinguished ancestor who had founded the clan.

The Gaelic-Irish form of the name Kelly, for example, is Ó Ceallaigh, or O'Kelly, indicating descent from an original 'Ceallaigh', with the 'O' denoting 'grandson of.' The name was later anglicised to Kelly.

The prefix 'Mac' or 'Mc', meanwhile, as with the clans of the Scottish Highlands, denotes 'son of.'

Although the Irish clans had much in common with their Scottish counterparts, one important difference lies in what are known as 'septs', or branches, of the clan.

Septs of Scottish clans were groups who often bore an entirely different name from the clan name but were under the clan's protection.

In Ireland, septs were groups that shared the same name and who could be found scattered throughout the four provinces of Ulster, Leinster, Munster, and Connacht.

The 'golden age' of the Gaelic-Irish clans, infused as their veins were with the blood of Celts, pre-dates the Viking invasions of the eighth and ninth centuries and the Norman invasion of the twelfth century, and the sacred heart of the country was the Hill of Tara, near the River Boyne, in County Meath.

Known in Gaelic as 'Teamhar na Rí', or Hill of Kings, it was the royal seat of the 'Ard Rí Éireann', or High King of Ireland, to whom the petty kings, or chieftains, from the island's provinces were ultimately subordinate.

It was on the Hill of Tara, beside a stone pillar known as the Irish 'Lia Fáil', or Stone of Destiny, that the High Kings were inaugurated and, according to legend, this stone would emit a piercing screech that could be heard all over Ireland when touched by the hand of the rightful king.

The Hill of Tara is today one of the island's main tourist attractions.

Opposition to English rule over Ireland, established in the wake of the Cambro-Norman invasion, broke out frequently and the harsh solution adopted by the powerful forces of the Crown was to forcibly evict the native Irish from their lands.

These lands were then granted to Protestant colonists, or 'planters', from Britain.

Many of these colonists, ironically, came from Scotland and were the descendants of the original 'Scotti', or 'Scots', who gave their name to Scotland after migrating there in the fifth century A.D., from the north of Ireland.

Colonisation entailed harsh penal laws being imposed on the majority of the native Irish population, stripping them practically of all of their rights.

The Crown's main bastion in Ireland was Dublin and its environs, known as the Pale, and it was the dispossessed peasantry who lived outside this Pale, desperately striving to eke out a meagre living.

It was this that gave rise to the modern-day expression of someone or something being 'beyond the pale'.

Attempts were made to stamp out all aspects of the ancient Gaelic-Irish culture, to the extent that even to bear a Gaelic-Irish name was to invite discrimination.

This is why many Gaelic-Irish names were anglicised with, for example, and noted above, Ó Ceallaigh, or O'Kelly, being anglicised to Kelly.

Succeeding centuries have seen strong revivals of Gaelic-Irish consciousness, however, and this has led to many families reverting back to the original form of their name, while the language itself is frequently found on the fluent tongues of an estimated 90,000 to 145,000 of the island's population.

Ireland's turbulent history of religious and political strife is one that lasted well into the twentieth century, a landmark century that saw the partition of the island into the twenty-six counties of the independent Republic of

Ireland, or Eire, and the six counties of Northern Ireland, or Ulster.

Dublin, originally founded by Vikings, is now a vibrant and truly cosmopolitan city while the proud city of Belfast is one of the jewels in the crown of Ulster.

It was Saint Patrick who first brought the light of Christianity to Ireland in the fifth century A.D.

Interpretations of this Christian message have varied over the centuries, often leading to bitter sectarian conflict – but the many intricately sculpted Celtic Crosses found all over the island are symbolic of a unity that crosses the sectarian divide.

It is an image that fuses the 'old gods' of the Celts with Christianity.

All the signs from the early years of this new millennium indicate that sectarian strife may soon become a thing of the past – with the Irish and their many kinsfolk across the world, be they Protestant or Catholic, finding common purpose in the rich tapestry of their shared heritage.

Chapter two:
City of the Tribes

While there is an Irish Gaelic version of the name, 'Seoighe', its origins lie on the plains of Normandy while bearers of the surname Joyce who settled in Ireland hailed from the valleys and mountains of Wales.

Further confusing the early history of the name is that it has two possible derivations.

One is that it is derived from the Norman-French 'Josse', in turn derived from the Latin 'guadere', meaning 'joyous'.

On a rather more aristocratic and martial level, another theory is that it derives from the ancient Breton name 'Iodac', itself derived from 'Iudh', meaning 'lord'.

It was certainly in martial form that the Joyces first arrived in Ireland in the late twelfth century and, more than 100 years before, on the shores of England – in the armed retinue of William, Duke of Normandy, better known to posterity as William the Conqueror.

Defeating Harold II, the last Anglo-Saxon king of England, in the battle of Hastings in 1066, the Normans lost no time in imposing and consolidating their power, rewarding their followers such as the Joyces with land taken from their defeated foes.

The tentacles of Norman power also reached into Wales

and it was here, in the Glamorganshire region, that the Joyces were granted land and assimilated with the native Celtic culture.

They also assimilated the ancient Celtic culture of Ireland, but this was only after they had brought fire and sword to the island they had invaded.

The Cambro- Norman invasion of Ireland was to prove to be one of the most significant events in the island's turbulent history, and the main reason for its success can be found in the opposing political and military interests that then held sway throughout the divided land.

Ireland was far from united, split up as it was into territories ruled over by squabbling chieftains who ruled as kings in their own right – and this inter-clan rivalry worked to the advantage of the invaders.

In a series of bloody conflicts one chieftain, or minor king, would occasionally gain the upper hand over his rivals, and by 1156 the most powerful was Muirchertach MacLochlainn, king of the O'Neills.

The equally powerful Rory O'Connor, king of the province of Connacht, opposed him but he increased his power and influence by allying himself with Dermot MacMurrough, king of Leinster.

MacLochlainn and MacMurrough were aware that the main key to the kingdom of Ireland was the thriving trading port of Dublin that had been established by invading Vikings, or Ostmen, in 852 A.D.

The city was taken by the combined forces of the Leinster and Connacht kings, but when MacLochlainn died the Dubliners rose up in revolt and overthrew the unpopular MacMurrough.

A triumphant Rory O'Connor entered Dublin and was later inaugurated as Ard Rí, but MacMurrough was not one to humbly accept defeat.

He appealed for help from England's Henry II in unseating O'Connor, an act that was to radically affect the future course of Ireland's fortunes.

The English monarch agreed to help MacMurrough, but distanced himself from direct action by delegating his Norman subjects in Wales with the task.

With an eye on rich booty, plunder, and lands, they were only too eager to obey their sovereign's wishes and furnish aid to MacMurrough.

MacMurrough crossed the Irish Sea to Bristol, where he rallied powerful barons such as Robert Fitzstephen and Maurice Fitzgerald to his cause, along with Gilbert de Clare, Earl of Pembroke, and also known as Strongbow.

The mighty Norman war machine moved into action in 1169, and so fierce and disciplined was their onslaught on the forces of Rory O'Connor and his allies that by 1171 they had captured Dublin and other strategically important territories.

It was now that a nervous Henry II began to take cold feet over the venture, realising that he may have created a rival in the form of a separate Norman kingdom in Ireland.

He landed on the island, near Waterford, at the head of a large army in October of 1171 with the aim of curbing the power of his Cambro-Norman barons.

Protracted war between the king and his barons was averted, however, when the barons submitted to the royal will, promising homage and allegiance in return for holding the territories they had conquered in the king's name.

Henry also received the submission and homage of many of the Irish chieftains, tired as they were with internecine warfare and also perhaps realising that as long as they were rivals and not united they were no match for the powerful forces the English Crown could muster.

English dominion over Ireland was ratified through the Treaty of Windsor of 1175, under the terms of which those chieftains who had submitted to his royal will were allowed to rule territory unoccupied by the Normans in the role of a vassal of the king.

Thomas de Joise, or Joyce, the first recorded Joyce in Ireland, had been among the ambitious Normans who had joined Strongbow's invasion force and, as a reward for his services, he and his retainers were granted lands in the province of Connacht, on the borders of present-day Co. Galway and Co. Mayo, in the west of the island.

Even to this day an area of Connemara, in Co. Galway, is known as Joyce's Country, while Renvyle House, previously one of their forbidding strongholds, now performs a rather more peaceful function as a hotel.

But it was in Galway city itself that the Joyces were destined to achieve fame and not an inconsiderable amount of fortune – as members of the celebrated Fourteen Tribes of Galway.

Apart from the Joyces, these fourteen tribes, or families, who came to dominate the life of the city and surrounding area for a period that spanned several hundred years, included the originally Norman families of Ath, Blake, Bodkin, Browne, Deane, Ffont, Ffrench, Lynch, Martyn, Morris, Skerret, and the native Irish families of Kirwan and D'Arcy, or Darcy.

The influence of these fourteen merchant families on the life of Galway was so profound that even today it is known as The City of the Tribes.

Situated as it is on the west coast of Ireland and overlooking Galway Bay, Galway city was an ideal location for lucrative trade with not only continental Europe, but also the West Indies – and this was a trade carried on with great skill by the Joyces and the other thirteen members of the fourteen tribes.

They came to dominate not only the wealth of the city and a great expanse of the surrounding area, but also the civic government; this power was consolidated in 1484 when England's Richard III granted them complete control over their affairs.

One famous anecdote that illustrates Galway's pre-eminence in these times concerns a visitor from foreign shores who naively assumed that Ireland was part of Galway, rather than Galway a part of Ireland.

An elite group, the tribes were, for a time at least, loyal to the English Crown and were described by many as belonging to the class known as 'Old English' – but the Joyces were not so aloof that they shunned marriage with 'outsiders.'

It is known, for example, that marriage alliances were made with the sept of the ancient Irish O'Brien clan who were of the illustrious line of the Princes of Thomond.

Ironically, loyalty to the Crown and gradual assimilation of native Irish culture – and in particular their devotion to the Roman Catholic faith – would sow the seeds for the eventual downfall of the Joyces and their fellow merchant families.

Chapter three:

Legends of the ring

The twelfth century Norman invasion of Ireland and the subsequent domination over the centuries of the English Crown had served to create three separate 'Irelands'.

There were the territories of the privileged families such as the Joyces, the Ireland of the disaffected Gaelic-Irish, and the Pale – comprised of Dublin itself and a substantial area of its environs ruled over by an English elite.

A simmering cauldron of discontent and resentment had been created – one that boiled over periodically in orgies of bloodshed and mayhem.

Fuelling the discontent was not only the arbitrary treatment by the English Crown of the native Irish, but also families such as the Joyces, who had previously proven loyal.

In this opposition to the Crown, the Joyces and many others found common cause with the native Irish, forging a common and proud Irish identity.

The cauldron of discontent boiled over in 1641 in the form of a rebellion by the Catholic landowners against the English Crown's policy of settling, or 'planting' loyal Protestants on Irish land.

This policy had started during the reign from 1491 to 1547 of Henry VIII, whose Reformation effectively outlawed the established Roman Catholic faith throughout his dominions – something that was anathema to loyal Catholic families such as the Joyces.

The settlement of loyal Protestants in Ireland continued throughout the subsequent reigns of Elizabeth I, James I (James VI of Scotland), and Charles I.

In the insurrection that exploded in 1641, at least 2,000 Protestant settlers were massacred at the hands of Catholic landowners and their native Irish peasantry, while thousands more were stripped of their belongings and driven from their lands to seek refuge where they could.

Terrible as the atrocities were against the settlers, subsequent accounts became greatly exaggerated, serving to fuel a burning desire on the part of Protestants for revenge against the rebels. Tragically for Ireland, this revenge became directed not only against the rebels, but Catholics such as the Joyces in general.

The English Civil War intervened to prevent immediate action against the rebels, but following the execution of Charles I in 1649 and the consolidation of the power of England's fanatically Protestant Oliver Cromwell, the time was ripe for revenge.

The Lord Protector, as he was named, descended on Ireland at the head of a 20,000-strong army that landed at Ringford, near Dublin, in August of 1649.

He had three main aims: to quash all forms of rebellion, to 'remove' all Catholic landowners who had taken part in the rebellion, and to convert the Irish to the Protestant faith.

An early warning of the terrors that were in store came when the northeastern town of Drogheda was stormed and taken in September and between 2,000 and 4,000 of its inhabitants killed, including priests who were summarily put to the sword.

Galway City had been a rebel stronghold and was accordingly besieged and forced into surrender in April of 1652.

During the siege the canny merchants such as the Joyces had refused to either join in its defence or take Cromwell's side – and it was this united stance of the fourteen merchant families that earned them the derogatory title coined by Cromwell's troopers of 'the fourteen tribes.'

Rather than being offended, however, the 'tribes' adopted the name as a badge of honour and defiance.

Honour was all they had left, however, as they were systematically stripped of their lands and ousted from their position of power and influence in favour of Protestants.

Their fortunes were briefly restored on the Restoration of the Catholic Stuart monarch Charles II in 1660, but all was lost following what is known as the Glorious Revolution that brought William of Orange and his wife, Mary, to the throne.

An attempt to restore James II (James VII of Scotland) ended in disaster at the battle of the Boyne in July of 1690, followed by further Jacobite defeats at Aughrim, Galway, and Limerick, the following year.

The Joyces and the other members of the Fourteen

Tribes never recovered, but their legacy endures, while the Joyces can lay claim to another legacy that has become deeply embedded in Irish culture.

This comes in the form of the famous Claddagh ring, named after the small Galway fishing village of Claddagh.

There are at least three different legends concerning the origins of the ring, believed to have been first produced on a large scale during the reign from 1662 to 1694 of Queen Mary II – although its unique design is believed to stretch back further. The ring features two hands clasping a heart, surmounted by a crown, and is said to be symbolic of love – represented by the heart – of friendship – represented by the hands – and of loyalty – represented by the crown.

This gave rise to the expression associated with the Claddagh ring of: 'With these hands I give you my heart and I crown it with my love.'

By tradition, the way in which the ring is worn signifies to strangers the romantic status of the wearer.

When worn on the right hand with the heart facing outward, it signifies the wearer's heart is 'open' and that they are not romantically attached to anyone.

When worn with the heart facing inward, it indicates the wearer's heart has been 'captured' by someone.

Worn on the ring finger of the left hand, with the heart facing outward, it indicates the wearer is engaged to be married, while worn with the heart facing inward is an indication that they are married.

One of the legends concerning the ring's mysterious origin concerns Margareth Joyce, a lady of Galway city who married a wealthy Spanish merchant by the name of Domingo de Rona.

She settled with him in his native Spain but when he died, leaving her his considerable fortune, she returned to Galway where, in 1596 she married Oliver Ogffrench, mayor of the city.

Margareth is then said to have used her inherited wealth to fund the construction of bridges throughout Connacht, and as a reward for this by a benevolent providence an eagle dropped the Claddagh ring into her lap.

This legend has curious parallels with another Galway legend of a crusader who returned from the Holy Land and used his wealth to build the walls of Galway city – wealth that had come to him after an eagle showed him where treasure was buried.

Another legend of the ring's origins concerns a prince who wanted to marry a beautiful young maid and, to prove to her father that his intentions towards his daughter were honourable, he fashioned the Claddagh ring as an enduring symbol of his love and devotion.

The legend that appears to have the greatest degree of historical accuracy, however, concerns Richard Joyce, a native of Galway city who in his youth left to seek his fortune in the West Indies, planning to return to marry his childhood sweetheart.

Moorish pirates attacked his ship en route, and Joyce was sold as a slave to a goldsmith in Algiers.

Apprenticed to his master, he became adept in the art of goldsmithing and when, in 1689, the provincial government in Algiers resolved to free all British slaves, his master offered him a share of his wealth and his daughter's hand in marriage if he would remain.

Joyce's heart lay in Galway, however, and he returned to marry his sweetheart – presenting her with the Claddagh ring he had skilfully and lovingly fashioned for her while still a slave.

It is known that one of the first acts of William of Orange when he took the throne as William III was to demand the release of all his subjects who were captives of the Moors.

One reliable Irish historical source notes that among the captives who were released was 'a young man of the name of Joyes, a native of Galway, who, fourteen years before, was captured on his passage to the West Indies by an Algerian Corsair.'

'Joyes', or Joyce, according to the source, had been bought by a wealthy Turk who trained him in the art of goldsmithing, a trade to which he successfully turned on his return to Galway.

In later centuries the crown on the Claddagh ring became identified by many Irish Republicans as a symbol of the British Crown – and accordingly designed their own ring, minus the crown, and known today as the Fenian Claddagh.

Chapter four:

On the world stage

Generations of Joyces have achieved, and continue to achieve, celebrity in a diverse range of fields.

An exotic blend of Irish, Welsh, and Spanish blood coursed through the veins of the American actress **Alice Joyce**, known as 'The Madonna of the Screen'.

Born Alice Joyce Brown in Kansas City, Missouri, in 1890 she was a star of mainly the silent movie era. Best known for her role in *The Green Goddess*, she died in 1955.

Born in Berkley, Virginia, in 1893, **Peggy Joyce** gained fame and celebrity both on and off the stage, not least for her six marriages and divorces to wealthy men.

She was born Marguerite Upton, and 'Joyce' was the surname of her second and third husbands respectively.

She first hit the Broadway stage in 1917, appearing with the celebrated *Ziegfeld Follies*, and through her succession of rich husbands she was at one time the owner of the Portuguese Diamond, one of the most expensive diamonds in the world.

Her many off-stage excesses and scandalous affairs led to her even being incorporated in the lyrics to songs, including the Rodgers and Hart *I've Got Five Dollars*.

An actress of rather less notoriety, but famous none the

less, is **Brenda Joyce**, the American actress who was born Betty Leabo in Excelsior Springs, Missouri, in 1912.

Appearing in a number of B-movies, she is best remembered as one of the actresses to have played Jane in the *Tarzan* series of films.

Born in London in 1927, **Yootha Joyce**, who died in 1980, was the star of a number of British television sitcoms in the 1970s, including *Man About The House* and *George and Mildred*, while **Elaine Joyce**, born in Kansas City, Missouri, in 1945, is the American actress who has appeared in a number of American television series, including *The Young and the Restless* and *Days of Our Lives*.

An actress of stage, screen, and television, **Ella Joyce**, born Cherron Hoye, in Chicago in 1954 has an impressive number of stage credits that include the character of Lily Ann Green in *Crumbs From the Table of Joy*, while across the Atlantic **Emily Joyce**, born in 1970, is the English actress who, in addition to performing with the Royal Shakespeare Company, has appeared in a number of British television sitcoms and crime series.

Also on the stage, **Ryan Joyce**, born in Hamilton, Ontario, is the award-winning Canadian magician and illusionist.

In the world of commerce, **David Joyce**, born in Sheffield, Massachusetts, in 1825, was a wealthy lumber baron and industrialist whose vast fortune was inherited on his death in 1904 by **Beatrice Joyce Kean**.

She put the money to good use in later years, using it to establish the charitable **Joyce Foundation** in 1948.

Based in Chicago and operating mainly in the Great Lakes region, it supports not only a vast range of environmental, educational, and cultural institutions, but also funds research into reducing gun deaths and injuries.

Another prominent supporter of a number of charities is the Canadian multi-millionaire **Ron Joyce**.

Born in 1930 and raised in Tatamagouche, Nova Scotia, he is the co-founder of the Tim Hortons donut chain, and was admitted to the Order of Canada in 1992 for his charitable work.

In the frequently cut-throat political sphere, **Barnaby Joyce**, born in 1967, is the National Party of Australia politician who, at the time of writing, is a member of the Australian Senate, representing Queensland.

Eric Joyce, born in 1960 in Perth, Scotland, is a British Labour Party politician who, at the time of writing, represents the constituency of Falkirk in the House of Commons.

From the hurly burly of party politics to the rather more serene realm of music, **Eileen Joyce**, born in Zeehan, Tasmania, in 1912, was the highly accomplished Australian pianist who first made her debut in 1930 at a Henry Wood promenade concert in London.

The daughter of an Irish father and a Spanish mother, she was able to fund her expensive musical studies in

Europe only thanks to the unstinting efforts of her far from wealthy parents and the generosity of the people of Western Australia.

She toured the world with a number of leading orchestras and contributed soundtracks to several films – most notably as the soloist in the Rachmaninoff second piano concerto used in the 1945 film *Brief Encounter*.

In contemporary times, **Mike Joyce**, born in Manchester in 1963, was the drummer with the '80s British band *The Smiths* and who has since performed with artistes such as the Irish singer Sínéad O'Connor.

Robert Dwyer Joyce, born in Glenosheen, Co. Limerick, in 1830, is remembered not only as a gifted poet, but as having played a vital role in collecting and rescuing from obscurity a number of old Irish songs.

He also wrote many of his own airs, and these were incorporated in the famous *Petrie Collection of the Native Music of Ireland*, published in 1855.

His poems include *The Boys of Wexford*, *The Blacksmith of Limerick*, and *The Wind that Shakes the Barley* – the title of a 2006 Ken Loach film.

In contemporary times, **Trevor Joyce**, born in Dublin in 1947, is the Irish poet who in 1967 co-founded the *New Writers' Press* in Dublin.

Arguably the most famous Joyce, certainly in the world of literature, is Séamus Seoighe, better known as the writer **James Joyce**, born in Rathgar, Dublin, in 1882.

He left for Paris after graduating in modern languages from University College, Dublin, in 1903, but returned a few months later.

Eking out a precarious living as a book reviewer and teacher he eventually eloped to the continent a year later with a chambermaid by the name of Nora Barnacle.

He returned often to Dublin, but most of his life was spent on the continent, particularly in Switzerland.

Despite his rather bohemian lifestyle, his literary output was impressive to the extent that he is now ranked as having been among the most influential writers of the twentieth century and a leading exponent of what is known as the modernist novel.

His famous works include *Dubliners*, published in 1914, *A Portrait of the Artist as a Young Man* (1916), *Ulysses* (1922) and *Finnegans Wake*, published in 1939.

Joyce died after surgery for a perforated ulcer in Zurich, Switzerland, in 1941 – ten years after he had finally married Nora, who died in 1951; their son, George, died in 1976.

In contemporary times, **Graham Joyce**, born in Coventry, is an English author in the genre of speculative fiction, for which he has won a World Fantasy Award, while **Brenda D. Joyce** is a best-selling author of romantic novels.

Born in New York in 1963, she wrote a novella when she was aged 16 and her first novel, *Innocent Fire*, was published nine years later.

Also in the world of the creative arts, **William Joyce**,

born in 1957, is the American writer, filmmaker, and illustrator whose many creations have included characters for the *Toy Story* movie.

In the highly competitive arena of sport, an American baseball great was **Bill Joyce**, born in St Louis in 1865.

As a third baseman, he played with teams that included the Brooklyn Wonders, Boston Reds, Brooklyn Grooms, Washington Senators, and New York Giants, who he also managed for a time.

Also on the baseball field is **James A. Joyce III**, the Major League umpire who was born in Toledo, Ohio, in 1955.

A former star of ice hockey is **Bob Joyce**, born in Saint John, New Brunswick, in 1966. In addition to the Winnipeg Jets, Joyce also played for the Boston Bruins and the Washington Capitals.

On the cricket pitch, **Ed Joyce** is the talented left-handed batsman and occasional right-arm bowler who was born in Dublin in 1978, while **Michael Joyce**, born in Santa Monica, California, in 1973 is the former American tennis player who, at the time of writing, coaches female tennis star Maria Sharapova.

Taking to the swimming pool, **Kara Lynn Joyce**, born in Brooklyn, New York, in 1985 is the swimmer who won silver medals for the U.S. in the 4x100m Freestyle Relay and the 4x100m Medley Relay at the 2004 Olympics in Athens.

A particularly notorious Joyce was **William Joyce**, born in New York in 1906 to an Irish father and an English mother.

The family returned to Galway, in Ireland, in Joyce's childhood, and later to England, where Joyce joined the British Union of Fascists in 1932.

On the outbreak of war, facing arrest and detention as a Nazi sympathiser, he and his wife fled to Germany and he became a radio propagandist for Germany's English service.

Dubbed Lord Haw-Haw by his mocking British listeners, he was captured after the war and, found guilty of treason, hanged in 1946.

Key dates in Ireland's history from the first settlers to the formation of the Irish Republic:

circa 7000 B.C.	Arrival and settlement of Stone Age people.
circa 3000 B.C.	Arrival of settlers of New Stone Age period.
circa 600 B.C.	First arrival of the Celts.
200 A.D.	Establishment of Hill of Tara, Co. Meath, as seat of the High Kings.
circa 432 A.D.	Christian mission of St. Patrick.
800-920 A.D.	Invasion and subsequent settlement of Vikings.
1002 A.D.	Brian Boru recognised as High King.
1014	Brian Boru killed at battle of Clontarf.
1169-1170	Cambro-Norman invasion of the island.
1171	Henry II claims Ireland for the English Crown.
1366	Statutes of Kilkenny ban marriage between native Irish and English.
1529-1536	England's Henry VIII embarks on religious Reformation.
1536	Earl of Kildare rebels against the Crown.
1541	Henry VIII declared King of Ireland.
1558	Accession to English throne of Elizabeth I.
1565	Battle of Affane.
1569-1573	First Desmond Rebellion.
1579-1583	Second Desmond Rebellion.
1594-1603	Nine Years War.
1606	Plantation' of Scottish and English settlers.
1607	Flight of the Earls.
1632-1636	Annals of the Four Masters compiled.
1641	Rebellion over policy of plantation and other grievances.
1649	Beginning of Cromwellian conquest.
1688	Flight into exile in France of Catholic Stuart monarch James II as Protestant Prince William of Orange invited to take throne of England along with his wife, Mary.
1689	William and Mary enthroned as joint monarchs; siege of Derry.
1690	Jacobite forces of James defeated by William at battle of the Boyne (July) and Dublin taken.

1691	Athlone taken by William; Jacobite defeats follow at Aughrim, Galway, and Limerick; conflict ends with Treaty of Limerick (October) and Irish officers allowed to leave for France.
1695	Penal laws introduced to restrict rights of Catholics; banishment of Catholic clergy.
1704	Laws introduced constricting rights of Catholics in landholding and public office.
1728	Franchise removed from Catholics.
1791	Foundation of United Irishmen republican movement.
1796	French invasion force lands in Bantry Bay.
1798	Defeat of Rising in Wexford and death of United Irishmen leaders Wolfe Tone and Lord Edward Fitzgerald.
1800	Act of Union between England and Ireland.
1803	Dublin Rising under Robert Emmet.
1829	Catholics allowed to sit in Parliament.
1845-1849	The Great Hunger: thousands starve to death as potato crop fails and thousands more emigrate.
1856	Phoenix Society founded.
1858	Irish Republican Brotherhood established.
1873	Foundation of Home Rule League.
1893	Foundation of Gaelic League.
1904	Foundation of Irish Reform Association.
1913	Dublin strikes and lockout.
1916	Easter Rising in Dublin and proclamation of an Irish Republic.
1917	Irish Parliament formed after Sinn Fein election victory.
1919-1921	War between Irish Republican Army and British Army.
1922	Irish Free State founded, while six northern counties remain part of United Kingdom as Northern Ireland, or Ulster; civil war up until 1923 between rival republican groups.
1949	Foundation of Irish Republic after all remaining constitutional links with Britain are severed.